In the Kitchen

Let's Make Pizza

By Mary Hill

Children's Press®
A Division of Scholastic Inc.
New York / Toronto / London / Auckland / Sydney
Mexico City / New Delhi / Hong Kong
Danbury, Connecticut

Photo Credits: Cover and all photos by Maura B. McConnell
Contributing Editor: Jennifer Silate
Book Design: Mindy Liu

Library of Congress Cataloging-in-Publication Data

Hill, Mary, 1977-
Let's make pizza / by Mary Hill.
    p. cm. — (In the kitchen)
  Includes index.
  Summary: A girl and her father go through the steps involved in making a
pizza.
  ISBN 0-516-23959-7 (library binding) — ISBN 0-516-24020-X (paperback)
  1. Pizza—Juvenile literature. [1. Pizza.] I. Title.

TX770.P58 H55 2002
641.8'24--dc21

2002001406

Contents

My name is Shari.

My dad and I are
making **pizza**.

First, Dad puts **sauce** on the **dough**.

He covers the dough with sauce.

Next, I put cheese
on top of the sauce.

I like cheese, so I put
on a lot.

I want **pepperoni** on my pizza.

I put **slices** of pepperoni all over the pizza.

Dad puts **green peppers** on our pizza.

I like them, too.

13

Now, Dad puts the pizza in the hot oven.

15

The pizza is done.

Dad cuts it.

How many slices are there?

There are eight slices.

Dad and I each take one.

19

Our pizza is very good.

I think I will have another slice!

21

New Words

dough (**doh**) a soft, sticky mixture of flour, water, and
other things, used to make bread, cookies, muffins,
and other food

green peppers (**green pep**-urz) green,
hollow vegetables

pepperoni (pep-ur-**oh**-nee) a spicy meat

pizza (**peet**-suh) a flat pie made of dough that is
topped with sauce, cheese, and more

sauce (**sawss**) a thick liquid used as a topping
on foods

slices (**sliss**-uz) thin, flat pieces cut from
something larger

To Find Out More

Books

Hold the Anchovies!: A Book about Pizza
by Shelley Rotner
Orchard Books

Pizza Fun: Ten Delicious Pizzas for Children to Make!
by Judy Bastyra
Larousse Kingfisher Chambers

Web Site

KidChef
http://www.kidchef.com
Play games and learn about food and cooking on this Web site.

Index

About the Author
Mary Hill writes and edits children's books from her home in Maryland.

Reading Consultants
Kris Flynn, Coordinator, Small School District Literacy, The San Diego County Office of Education

Shelly Forys, Certified Reading Recovery Specialist, W.J. Zahnow Elementary School, Waterloo, IL

Sue McAdams, Former President of the North Texas Reading Council of the IRA, and Early Literacy Consultant, Dallas, TX